Odder Still

Odder Still

Poems: Jim Culleny

Lena's Basement Press

Books may be purchased in quantity and/or special sales by
contacting the publisher, Lena's Basement Press, at
PO Box 317, Conway, MA 01341; 413-522-9725,
or by email at: lenasbasementpress@comcast.net

Published by:

LBP *Lena's Basement Press*
Conway, MA 01341

Interior & cover design and production:
Andrea Schettino, Andrea@ArtigianoJewelbox.com
Cover art: pen & ink by Jim Culleny
Editing: Marylou Dee
ISBN: 978-0-692-35154-3
10 9 8 7 6 5 4 3 2 1
1. Poetry
First Edition
Printed in USA

*For Pat
and my daughters Jessie, Jecca, Leah and Ashly*

Contents

Foreword

At their heart Culleny's poems are always probing, speculative and filled with nostalgia, wonder and yearning, poems that instantly elevate and connect with the reader. Even his serious themes questioning mankind's failings, lack of concern about the destruction of the planet, or mankind's avaricious need to conquer and control can be both elegiac and ironically humorous. Almost all of his poems are instructive, but not didactic, and offer the reader the often sought epiphany that fires up the minds and hearts of all who read him.

Culleny is also a musician: each poem's music, its cadences, repetitions and variations provides the reader with greater uplifting, complementing and enriching each piece.

Culleny's voice is rich and warmly engaging. Readers who wish to access vocal performances of his poems and songs can link into them at this site: https://soundcloud.com/jim-culleny.

–Mary Lou Dee

Odder Still

As odd as it is that the moon comes up
behind the inelegant tree behind our house
over the dark mountain —grey-white
and silver-dollar like, a night eye
weeping silver— it's odder still to think
of a moon that never was

As odd as spring seems, fresh and crisp
as the salad before the salmon fillet
As odd as the salmon fillet itself seems,
pink upon my plate— it's odder still
to think, *no salmon,* and *spring
never was*

As odd as breathing this night air
cucumber cool into my lungs
with a vague taste of pine and
something else, maybe a wood fire
ablaze in a stove down the valley; as odd
as pine and burning wood seems, it's
odder still to think otherwise, now,
standing on two feet and good legs
and all the electricity I need to be
sparking, snapping, seeing—
as odd as all this seems,
otherwise seems odder still
to me

1

Another Piece of Eternity

Another Piece of Eternity

I'm peeling back a page reading a new day
by the light of a new sun

mom died years ago,
or was it yesterday?

I once read something similar by Camus
but was too new to understand that time bleeds
its dyes are not fast but run between years
and sometimes as in old cloth
the colors of time become homogeneous

    —but here's this day blaring like a fanfare
    from a new horn crisp as frost on glass
    its brink sharp as the edge of a blade
    slicing off another piece of eternity

Tao Meets $(E = mc^2)$

Heaven conforms to the Way (Tao). The Tao conforms to its own nature.
> *—Lao Tzu, Poet; 6th century BC*

Something unknown is doing we don't know what.
> *—Sir Arthur Eddington, Astrophysicist;*
> *26 centuries later*

I'm as left as I am right
as up as I am down
as in as I am out
as far as I am near

I'm loud as pianissimo
I'm bright as I am blind
as cool as caliente
as body as I am mind

I'm dark as I am light
as here as I am there
as seen as out of sight
depending upon your where

Long story short
I'm nuanced and mirrored
as $(E = mc^2)$

As the Minute Clicks

A new night and cool
—unlike June in Jersey
when I was green
but June anyway

anyway it comes
it's June
it's June
regardless of you

June then
June now
mid-evening
8:30 by the clock
—the night dark
almost

in the window the sky
glows grey behind
silhouetted trees

slate-skin clouds
which if seen from a jet
would billow bright
in the light of the torch
that makes us tick—

while underneath on
cloud-muffled earth what
makes us tick is a phantom
flame we imagine

we imagine it hints it's here
right now in June

Brandenburg Concertos
from the other room
fountain water falling
nearby from a stone frog's lips

car passing
cat darting

makes you wonder how
you're doing as the minute
clicks

Alarm

wake as much as possible
before you sleep

catch your breath while the sun's up
when in February after a snow
everything's so soaked with light
sleep is impossible
and all that's left is to catch a day
by an hour and do-si-do
in incandescence

forget about sleep and dreams
forget the doldrums and
wake to what the crows caw
cackling over carrion

    wake
to the wind's insistence that
moving-on is the way
the world works

    wake
    to its alarm

What About Today?

If when's the question

    ever's the answer

If when is the question:

    always

When?

    forever

When is yesterday?

    never

When's tomorrow?

    never

What about today?

    is

History

---

before a beginning
is the end of a another beginning

history's a tangled skein
not a straight-laid thread

it's full of knots of strands of varied weights
and counter-weights of light and lead

when teased apart we learn
who today has lost and who is winning

who is floating
who is falling

who is free, or who is hauling
someone else's freight

who can move, or who is in the vice
of someone else's sinning

Burning Bush

At twenty I danced the tops of walls
Nijinsky of the double top plate

bent in-two like an onion shoot
unbending up through an earthen gate

lifting sticks to be put in place
nailing their tails held against my boot

walking the wires of gravity's net
as a spider commands the filament web

hung in the crotch of the jamb of a door
between one post and its lintel head

From the crow's nest of my wall-top perch
poised to get the next piece set

in air as clear as a baby's thoughts
surveying homes unlived-in yet

fresh-footed, balanced, without a clue
assessing my recent work and worth:

the shades of studs plumb and true
lying like bars over up-turned earth

Sweatskin slickkening in the light
breath as sure as the bellows of god

biceps built by the truth of weight,
muscles doing their natural jobs:

arms of sinew, bone and grit
reaching to haul the next board up

to be lifted and laid wall to ridge
and fixed by hammer blows on steel

fueled by blasts of the burning bush
in the orchard of god that has ever spun

like the fire that made big Moses reel
the burning bush we call the sun

Add 30 Seconds

---

add 30 seconds to anytime,
what's that interval?

hell, double it
what's that?

have you ever had a day that lasts three
or one that goes so fast it's past —instantly?

are those durations short or long,
if hours mean anything?

subtract 5 hours from anytime
do we really think we've minced minutes?
as we tick them off are they really not there?

there's a continuum called now
outside of which is guesswork
because our instruments only work here
slice it anyway you want
it remains still,
whole
our clocks do not
affect it

now is never what it was before
because things change
and will change again, now,
not yesterday or tomorrow
it only happens now

now is the only thing we have to work with
now only knocks now

Which is Which or Who is Who

---

fruit fly brains
may be made to have memories
of where they've never flown

I'm like a fruit fly in this way
I remember things I'm not sure
but think I've known

events that may be dreams
or fictions so often told
they're recollections or
heart-breaking tales so well rehearsed
that empathetic neurons,
like the mushroom body
of a fruit fly brain,
are excited to the point of déjà vu
remembering an explicit past not mine but
one that may be known by you

hours that seem like yesterday
recalled as clearly
as if each sunrise you've seen
had been seen by me
each brilliant tinted crimson fall
each blazing summer
each fresh green spring recalled
as if they'd been interred
within a nest of neurons
dark as a womb
to be resurrected
by a universal heart
not so particular about

which is which or
who is who

Fire in the Brain

God is a fire in the brain Nijinsky said
which is as close to the truth as
anything a dancer might dance
with a bonfire burning in his head

God may put you in a trance
with the fluttering of cardinal wings
or with the way the moon looks
mounting the mountain's back
on the other side of the river
—a bright hole in the dark
a splinter of hope
a sliver

Sometimes beyond the blazing bars
of your incarceration you hallucinate stars

You surmise the sun's a substantiating eye
but fear that every distance is not near
(not close enough to make the untellable clear)

You dream days
You dream nights

Sometimes you lie without a clue
in the hour of the wolf
waiting for the wolf to bite

or for the blue to light
When it does you see crocuses

You taste a cloud of honeysuckle
that sweetly drifts across the yard
where at a certain spot
between the garden and the shed

you swear paradise is here
—precisely here where a skunk
shredded grass the night before
grubbing while you were in bed
grubbing with a skunky conflagration
in her head

God may burn a brain and brand it
God may shrink it or expand it

This is the bed in which
our ignorance reposes which,
by every blister on our brain,
is both a bed of coals
and roses

Same Difference

The Buddha's doctrine is thus proven:
nothing in this world is created.
          (Octavio Paz, per Dharmakirti)

Nothing in this world is created,
said Buddha looking into the bowl of a lotus

Nothing is created

In this lotus filled to the brim
is nothing which has been created

Nothing is created

From the bottom of this lotus brimming with nothing
but filled with hope open as a door

Nothing is created

Nothing in Buddha's lotus is created
This lotus has been overflowing always

Nothing is created

Something mounts the sky like a sun
wave by wave in no time ladened with light always

Uncreated

When I woke this morning it was
inundating Bald Mountain

Uncreated

When was it not created?
Could it have been

Uncreated?

Buddha suggests
Nothing is created

Buddha is
Uncreated

What created creation?
Nothing

or the
Unknown

same difference

The Pool of Buddha's Eyes

The asphalt of the walk to the door is black
but not as dark as the silence
of the concrete Buddha on the porch
as I climb the steps to work

The Buddha sits center on the top step
with a nascent nest in his hands,
his downcast eyes seeing
bits of straw a bird has brought
and placed as if it thought the safest site
to build this spring was in the lap
of a grey Buddha upon a porch
in a small town on a planet
in a galaxy among billions
in a small universe swimming
in the pool of Buddha's eyes

2

Rattling My Cage

Rattling my Cage

Are you looking at me? I say to the mountain
which moves as I guide the tiller down the row

But maybe it's not the mountain I address

Are you talking to me? I say to the pale moon
which sits upon the mountain like a ghost ball

But maybe the moon is not the ghost of this conversation

The Briggs and Stratton snorts. The tiller's deep-treaded
tires turn. The Buddha in the engine barks. The tines
lift the secret earth buried under tough sod

Are you overseeing me? I say to the crow
who stands off like an incriminating shadow

But the crow may not be the shade to whom I speak

Soon spinach will be sprouting in these rows
The prints I leave in the soil behind the tiller
will have been smoothed over by a rake

Are you reminding me of something?
I say to no one in particular

A Hole in the Banal

Socrates said to Glaucon, "The things we think we know are like shadows cast on the walls of a cave by a distant light of things unseen we do not know."

For L.

You called last night troubled.
Looking for something in particular
(a pink balloon shaped like the heart
of your long dead cousin)
you'd stumbled upon a hole in the banal:
a weakened spot in the thin skin of our conceits
stretched so taut over the otherworld
a hint of it broke through and pierced
your shell of rapt doing
and you glimpsed the truth of shades
that dance upon the walls of caves
to music most often unheard
under the rush of jets
behind the daily brushing of leaves against sky
drowned by the litanies of radios
made silent by the roar of willed tornadoes
blowing through the aisles of malls
muted by the fierce narcissism of war
the accumulation of stuff thrown up
as dikes to keep the unspeakable sea at bay
and you wondered if perhaps Socrates was right
So I recalled for you a day driving to Colrain
when a song bled from the dash
so filled with poignancy my heart broke too

and I sobbed from the steel arched bridge
where two rivers meet to the office door
remembering my mother,
my father, and Danny my autistic brother
hearing them hearing me sob
through a veil of ordinary tears and regret
saltier than the Dead Sea
This is where you and I meet, where we all meet,
on the beach of that sea, catching now and then
between surf and horizon glimpses of creatures
breaking through, breaching the membrane
between worlds unexpectedly
as we wonder how the dancing shadows
on cave walls can be true

Does Philosophy Matter

it's high summer
wild green thrusts itself
against the bounds
of clipped lawns
Huns of sumac
massed at a farm's edge
surge toward logical
rows of beets and
well-reasoned
ranks of peppers
ignoring the protocol
of invitation under
the wingspread
of a hawk clueless
about the theological
knots of Aquinas

—a hawk who can't imagine
the ontological argument,
who just wheels like
Gump's feather rising

and falling on whims
of wind scanning for lunch
without thinking I think,
therefore I am, being
without the anguish of Hamlet's
big question; someone whose
knowledge is written in cells

—a bird whose understanding
is unscorched by the burning of books
unscathed by the thoughts of the dead,
the ideologies of idiots,
the desperation to make sense
of what cannot be said

— someone snared nevertheless
in the terminal webs
of bi-pedal thinkers who
plumb and mine the shadows
in their heads

Better to Say Now

I almost didn't get up today
sleep

was so *I-want-to-stay-here-the-world-is-fucked*
but

there's still something blissful about breathing
and

notwithstanding what's all too typical in this world
I

opened my eyes and found you there
as

startlingly usual and knew that with you and our daughters
and

friends and the means to ambulate, see, hear, and help
I'd

miss a lot just sleeping, somnambulating, dreaming,
so

I threw back the covers and jumped into another
day

since chances may not be as abundant
in

the after-life or next-life if there are such things. Better to say,
Now

Posterity

      all that
      follows

every generation since Oldowan man chipped obsidian and flint
to make a stone ax to lay open the skull of an adversary
for food or turf, honing technique until

      at this end
      he's chipped them
      into ICBMs

posterity

the inner stuff of blind surge
the inclination of instinct
down a slippery slope

      the popped buds
      of hope
      or

whatever's survived
the gauntlet of a willful Demiurge
in which rank and ecstatic
blossoms collide

posterity

what morphs into the next thing

which unfolds from a chrysalis
and mounts the sky

> a lime Luna moth the color of bliss
> a bird that whistles, a bird that sings
> desire that will not desist
> the leading edge of everything

> the fruit it brings
my daughters now in the outer world
pushing on, pioneers

> a bird that whistles
> a bird that suffers
> a bird that sings

Breeze

微风

I dreamt I was dreaming in Chinese

I didn't understand my dream but its calligraphy was clear
as the silken brush of *breeze*
The characters, *Lao Tzu,* climbed behind my open eyes
but said as little as they could mounting nothing hill
obliquely vanishing between two skies
I came upon a Buddha sitting wise as a pictograph without a word,
silently loquacious, musical, mute, unheard as a muzzled mourning dove

In this dream I'm free of words and guile as Buddha's smile

That's All He Wrote

There, next to a begonia
whose rose-tinged leaves are burnished
succulent and still
my self is in a room
near a window in the sun
its feet upon a sill

—then, as now, it takes down
or makes up the tale of itself
in sight of the star above a pine
past noon remembering,
telling the story of itself
to itself, becoming itself,
spinning its character
from threads of old and new seconds
it stitches into its days and months
of turned-over leaves
(as clear as the nose on the face of itself
but strange too as it tells and tells)
who reads between the lines of itself
following the story's spell
back to the start of itself
in the beginning, before which
and beyond the last leaf,
there's nothing to denote
—that's all he wrote

Trick Question

–A friend asked, "Jim how are you —really?"
Must be a trick question

Not a trick by the asker
but trick by
my inner magician,
my personal convoluter,
my lithe prevaricator
who first teased Eve
under a tree
with the acid, orange
kumquat of knowledge
which he bounced
upon his forked tongue
and upon which Eve
and her shifty lover
sadly choked

The question,
How are you, *really?*
is impossible for a fake
to bear
To answer would be
to mock God
who sees through spin
no matter how sincere

Better to say,
Gooder 'n some
Better to say,
Badder 'n others
Better to say,
A mixed bag complex.
A hick in a zoot suit
A pansy in a bucket
of muck

I keep up appearances
I do my thing

I balance odds and ends
as best I can

I go not where the four
winds blow

You want the naked truth?
Let me think about it 'cause
I don't know

Un About

---

snow glittered to the wavelengths of a streetlamp
on swells and bellies of the yard slope
down, across a white savannah
from asphalt to nirvana

at a window I stood looking out
forever in a moment
in today or yesterday or mañana
enmeshed, engaged, rapt
and un about

senseless to the dialogic loop ever playing in this headspace
of fruitless whys and how-comes, a chronic head case

stopped now   still   synchronized   void

empty   apophatic   absent   unalloyed

vacant as a black hole

silent as the innards of a whole note
vibrating to the rhythm of sixteenths

unmoored, unsyntaxed
adrift and tuned

until a plow truck threw its plume across the driveway
and I was back and bound again, too soon

In Has Tumbled Out

---

beyond the window: a wine-dark sea
first light hasn't touched the boundary birch

pre-dawn cocoon luxurious
silence in this sinner's church

rapt, and so devout, out has fallen in,
in has tumbled out

as I respire, without which
there'd be no coming no going
no out-to-in or in-to-out
no seeing, being, faith or doubt

levitating over town
a chalk balloon still hovers

it comes down to this:
day comes round, erratic bliss
furtive, pure, sometimes profound

day comes again,
a faithful moon, a lover

Say Something Obvious

The geometry of moonlight is triangular
Its pallid glow is whole, homogeneous and crisp,
never granular. Moon mates with Sun,
cries like a bell, her rings are ecstatic and annular

Under a condensing cloud you'll be singing in the rain
if you carry a tune while following your bliss
If it falls upon the skin of lovers it will hiss

We had a Harley once, too small to ride
to I L from N J, but we went anyway
Later, not even a kiss

The forearm muscles of the young,
their Palmaris Longus and Carpis Ulnaris,
are means to an end
they're not there for show, but to work
In the old they sometimes give sharp hints
of what's left to spend

Behind a blower in the snow
if the wind whips the plume just so
(colder bitter cheeks with every flake)
you may as well have been with Scott's expedition
in Antarctica freezing in determination
dying from mistake

There's good to be said for caution
and brashness too
                              reticence or passion
—you'll only know which one was called for
when the day is through

Tide

the way it
comes, goes,
surges, disappears,
a perfect metaphor
for shapes of time,
overused as *moon*
for that which vanishes
and reappears

quiet now, the wedding past,
too much so—
a house that buzzed
now hushed   silence loud   sharp
but slimmer than a midnight crescent

silence also
comes goes empties spills ebbs   fills
evaporates and billows like a cloud
above a sugarbush still
boiling down sweet water
for its essence

Tell me Something I Don't Know

Don't tell me the earth's a sphere
and the sun's kiss amounts to half-day
terminal bliss with a dark end
or that winters have to do with angles,
mystics have to do with angels
and lovers are about orbiting passions
that pulse like binary stars
across light years
and come in telescopes

Don't tell me the wind's a metaphor
for a longing to fill vacuums
that sometimes spit typhoons
or that cardinals seen
in the high reaches of cherry trees
are no more sublime than worms
who burrow among turnip roots
for a living

Don't tell me the chance of being
is equal to the odds of not being

—tell me something I don't know

Tell me how to weave
tomorrow into yesterday
without tangling, without
strangling today

Spirit Level

I've been a carpenter most of my life
and so have had occasion to use
what used to be called a spirit-level
but which today we call a level
–ditching spirit for the sake of efficiency
baby-with-bath-water-like
as we often do well past what's necessary
but the hole heaps up

this level is used to set things straight
with the plane of the horizon as in a beam
or plumb as with a stud to make sure
structure's right by spirit
you breathe deep and easy and hold the level
so the spirit bubble floats in the small arc of a glass flask
dead center which if placed upon a joist would say,
this floor is level

being on the level
good way to be

Muhheakantuck

The river that flows both ways
runs through my house

Sometimes called paradox
—called Muhheakantuck by the Lenape
who knew that reversals of time
are not unusual,
just often misunderstood by we-
who-walk-away-from-understanding

The river that flows both ways
has two sources
one in front and one behind. It flows from
two horizons and meets here
in the middle turbulently sometimes
but not always —only when I speak with
forked tongue. At all other times it
comes together silently as one

The river that flows both ways
is a god with two faces
—antipodal from beginning to end,
Janus (like Vishnu) drifts upon his raft
into the past and future at once
remembering and hoping

The river that flows both ways
is a mirror
whose face is a nexus as Alice knew
by walking through— call it Paradox,
a town, a place I lived once
in the time before this

The river that flows both ways
has nothing to do with imagination
or poetic conceits

The river that flows both ways
really falls from a high place
is caught by tides
and carried back into estuaries

The river that flows both ways
flows through my house;

like the Lenape
I call it
Muhheakantuck

What God Says

I place before you a bowl of evidence
but will never make you eat

Chance is what you're up against:
the only is of me you meet

You can pray until your tongues expire
and never know my heart's desire

I roll the future out mysteriously,
you trace my trail of crumbs through mires

You profusely write of who I am
as if I were like you a man

You cannot know the I of me
unless you crack the I of thee

In the light and in the gloom
I beat a drum and hum your tune

Atonement

Yom Kippur

To find the means to a mend

To try a new take to forsake a mistake

To unfold the past and straighten its bend

To un-muddy a pool and make it clear

To lift the flat rock of our self and let the sun do its work

To yank the inside out and give it some air

To make a whole man of the stuff of a jerk

To morph a long fall into a hairpin turn

To lance a boil and do what's best for us

To kindle the badly done and watch it burn

To unbury the past and make its corpse a Lazarus

To sew a split in one cloth, now two

To impossibly do what the humble do

To end a grudge and make us whole again

At one ment then

3

A Hole In Vincent's Head

A Hole In Vincent's Head

I'm looking through a hole in Van Gogh's head.

The hole I'm peering through is a painting some call Terrasse de Cafe.

It could be called Fire and Ice. Wonderful would be another apt name for it.

This piece of Vincent is a night sky hung with stellar lanterns near as lightposts,

as if the cosmos was just another canopy slightly beyond the one shielding the cafe.

Just a stone's throw beyond. Within spitting distance. Half a hair's breadth away.

Stars big as moons hang in this room in Vincent's skull. Stars ready as wet Cortlands

to be plucked from trees in orchards of exploding hydrogen.

Under the cafe canopy nano-figures repose upon cobbles of burning coals.

Sipping wine maybe; savoring oysters; sucking energy from supernovas.

Near and Far opposed as lovers in Vincent's embracing mind.

There and Here tangled beyond belief.

Capela Dos Ossos

—on the Church of Bones, Evora Portugal

We pray in a church of bones
in which skulls outline graceful arches
of low vaults and whose columns are ladders
of stacked femurs. We admire its capitals
of craniums

Its walls, unlike the idealizations
of Michelangelo, are not fantasies
romanced in fresco but the real thing:
the stony remnants of once-respiring
antiquity

We pray in a church of bones
whose windows look out
beneath an osseous calcium dome

Our chapel of once-articulating skeletons
—a reliquary of dreams—
rises over a promontory like a lighthouse
warning the world of muscle and bone,
spit and sweat, breath and blood
to steer clear of the promises of ghosts
and constantly sound to avoid being
beached in mud

We pray in a church of bones
We hope in a field of dreams
We hate or love between
unknown and unknown

Poets Talk Time

poets talk time
to get a handle on it
to hack a place to hold it
to turn it, to fold it
to climb it and mount it
to ride it, to flip it
to hide it, to turn it
to toy with and tip it
to wrench it, to rip it
apart to unlearn it,
to kill it, to burn it
to track it in the innards of clocks
to pick it apart like a crow on a corpse
to drill it to dig it to bore it
and finally, ignore it

but poets would do well to pour time
like water, or blood & wine
and savoring,
sip it

The Worker, Sisyphus

It's not so much the repetitive
rolling of the rock;
its hard weight against my skin
—we all bear our constant running

It's not the sweat or muscles
burning in my calves,
my flaming gastrocnemius
my toasted soleus
—father Adam was told this was coming

It's not so much my wrenched shoulders,
lacerated knees, abraded hands
or the endless throbbing of ankles
sprained by their turning again and again
in the small ruts beneath the rock
as I inch it up
—it's all in a day's work, as they say

It's not the back spasms
that seize up sometimes
like a stubborn mind
—such things are par for the course
in this tearful vale

It's not the danger of its rolling back
to flatten me under its planetary mass;
it's not the threatening heft of the thing
as I urge it up the incline
—we all live under an axe

It's not the wasted time
the eternal leisure lost
the laceration of days
the spent eternity
—eternities come and go

It's not the abjectness of my condition
—humiliation is only the next-to-worst thing
to bear

It's not what it means to have such
intimacy with my stone;
to know its subtle veining,
its lumps and concavities, its tiny fissures,
it's imperfect roundness, all of which
I see, blurred, through rivulets of sweat
—I've had plenty of time to get to know it well

And size is not the problem
Immensity does not scare me
—even what's huge can be overcome by tenacity

What rips my soul is the instant in which
this stone, at the precise moment of bitter success,
tumbles like one of Hannibal's elephants
from an alpine precipice to lodge always but
momentarily in chronic doldrums
until, restless, I must roll again

Good Poet

a good poet is subversive
—not to the point of blood in the streets
          necessarily

but to the point of burrowing beneath
his garden of conceits like an insistent vole
killing those weeds at their roots

everybody in this way
can walk in a good poet's
boots

ODDER STILL

Loophole

Abraham said to his father and his people:
"What are these images to whose worship you cleave?"
They said: "We found our fathers worshipping them."
He said: "Certainly you have been, you and your fathers, in
manifest error."
  –Koran, Chapter 21, verses 52-54

Warnings in the Hadith
to make no image of God
or man or animal
are no match for the loophole
function of the human mind
that overcomes
obstacles like certainty
and threats of hellfire
to make real any
object of longing
mystic or material
as can easily be seen
in the lovely, lyrical
portrait, the Tughra
(signature of Suleiman
the Magnificent),
disguised as calligraphy,
a loophole allowed in
Muhammad's line by men
who knew the futility
of banning beauty

4

—

With You

With You

Under a full moon

Under a luminous night sky under a full moon

Under stark black trees in the cold under
a luminous sky at night under a full moon

under stars unseen in light of the full moon
hung over a second sphere with an iron core

under a magma sea beneath twelve billion dancing human feet
upon a crust brittle and hard of granite and gneiss

under a humus bed black as oil
under fathoms of sea and sand and stone

Cenozoic remains pooled under
the smoke of burning pearls of wisdom
curling through skulls clouding
the march of mammals and millipedes

under a luminous sky at night under a full moon
radiating silver, under these stark black trees
in the midnight cold I walk with you

Intuition

stand close
closer
closest

sit beside me
close

so close the electricity
of our arms spark

you and I will be a pair of lovers

close closer closest

friends
too

Sugarphone

Your voice on the telephone
is sugar to my ears

Your electric breath nudging magnets,
eating miles as it comes –
meeting relays, swelling,
exciting antennae...
Your voice runs with light

It enters at absurd gates
convoluted to catch frequencies
of love and death; appendages
that on my young freshcut head
once stood out like pink wings

Now on this motel phone
buried in bedclothes they catch you,
or what of you electricity brings

Miles and geography disappear
Squeezed to bits by chips
you come juice-sweet, and ease
through the earpiece of this
sugarphone

Sure Thing

Expect nothing and nothing
will come bearing something
—sure thing
> *–Roshi Bob*

This is how the world began:
expecting nothing

but see how something
(a brilliant blazing ball
caroming off the tip of Kepler's cue)
breaks the horizon,
trails a crimson veil of light
which sets the sea afire
with fierce luminescence
and me with fierce delight

this is how it is:
the earth, without expectation,
became a seething knot of azurite,
it's nourishing greens and blues
spun from the cornucopia of nada
as if nothing's empty store
were a well of even more

this is how it was:
I sat upon a diner stool
elbows on the countertop
forearms straddling my book
like the legs of that Colossus
astride the harbor door of Rhodes
scanning the sea for future ghosts
and you came with carafe
and side of toast

and nothing—
nothing expected could compare
with your unanticipated eyes
and chestnut hair

Who gets the Thing
That Makes You Tick

The world goes round
One day you find someone who knows—
who gets the thing that makes you tick
gets it right and gets it quick

No words can tell the joy of this
You might as well be kindling in a fire,
rapt within its flame—

Enjoy the heat
Listen to your embers hiss

Blue Under Blue

We were sitting on a bench under blue
under the bush of a willow admiring her garden when
I saw an Indigo Bunting but didn't know it when I did

Look, I said,
a bluebird on the wall!

No, the fabulous near-turquoise of it,
its deep and tiny beyond-blueness makes it
an Indigo Bunting, she said, *if it's*
anything at all

It hopped, mysterious as one of the angels some say exist
and took off fluttering more beautifully than
the idea of fluttering

fluttering for real

took off into wisteria
like the idea of flying
(cubed at least)

Who thought that up, the flying?
-not to mention the wisteria
I said. Truth is

that's what we were both feeling
both thinking just then
seeing an Indigo Bunting so blue
under blue under willow
from our bench

Cold Sting

Last night under a full moon
under a threat of frost
we threw row covers over the kale

We stumbled from a pile near the tracks
with bins of river rocks
to weigh the covers down

Wind waved their white lightness
over the Red Russian and Lacinato
as if we were flagging Nature,
signaling *Ok, ok, you win again*

We laughed and mocked ourselves
for hauling stones so late in the day
in a black plastic bin among full-mooncast-shades
stumbling over clods of autumn-tilled rows
covering kale to save ourselves and the stuff of soup
from the cold sting of this newest
turn of the earth

Topology

I love the space of your soul
the way it tends up and out
like that wide field in Conway
near the sugarhouse
which one spring blossomed
with dandelions
so dense and profuse
its rising hump
in the morning sun
was a mound of gold
whose worth in brilliance
was more fabulous
than that most coveted ore

I love the coves and niches
of a soul that billows
like vapor through a sugarhouse roof,
through its cupola

—your sugarhouse soul
its volumes and transformations
its rich continuity
sweetens the shape of me

I love a soul that pushes
envelopes   I love
the edgy ellipse of your
horizon harrowing soul

a soul both
now and soon
here and there
turned in, turned out
which, if I follow its piper
and her Mobius band,
will lead me round

not to the place I was
but to the better side
of where I am

Over the Counter

I lean from behind Buber while
Thou serveth me caffeine and smile.

I know my elbows rest upon the sky.
O! the blue formica shines.

I see your red cheeks blare
in oval frame of hair.

Arthur stares me down.
He's an angry, sad, old,
ruddyfaced lecher. Alone.

He imagines you his young lover.
He pushes baked haddock past
tired lips.

The chrome coffee pitcher
belches water vapor.

It rises to your eyes
and there they are, cloud bourn,
as the brown liquid drops my buzz.

My soles float over the counter rail.

Never weaned from fantasy,
I want to nail down my shoes,
not wanting to trust romance:

Fool's paradise, I say.
Love cool reason.
I say, *do it alone. No.*

Oh, I'd love to do it right.
To give it up. Free
the hawks and doves and be slave
only to discovery.

A Simple Ontology

maybe flower petals are held to stems by thought
and the wind's a counter-thought that plucks
and places them elsewhere in the grass
to rest in contemplative resolution
beside the notion of a grub-pulling crow

maybe the wind itself is a palpable bright idea,
something about motion and the abhorrence of vacuums
something about coming and going,
about ferocity and stillness
about war and its absence

maybe the moon's the concept of fullness,
loss, abatement, regeneration from slivers,
hope at the hour of the wolf, the opposite of
darkness at the break of noon,
the upside of shadow

maybe Descartes had it right
and this, from horizon to horizon, is
a simple ontology,
an inherent daisy chain of ideas chasing its tail

regardless

one idea hatched in this synapse nest
is to harvest thought from thought
under a perception of blue
while the conception of breeze
riffles the hint of hair
and I place them
like dreams of plums
into the essence of basket
and give them
with the intention of love
to my belief
in the natural being
of you

Wakening

Facing Goliath

Like wound springs we wait inside a medic's room
my dearest friend and lover sits upon the table
we do the ritual things we do
we laugh against doom
like David with his stone
we do the tiny things we're able

The Surgeon Said

Some days I think
lies would serve us best
but this is just delusion
How could I choose
to spin what's real
with the wrench of imagination,
isn't that the definition of a fool?

Whatever it is it's here
so deal with it
(the surgeon said sorry
about the biopsy)

The Cardelaveo Abyss

Without you would be the
Cardelaveo Abyss

which is no place I know
or which even exists
unless by coincidence
because I just made it up
to convey the vast emptiness
I would know without you

Awakening in a 2 a.m. funk

What I was doing up
was being down
not in a dreadful sense
but in the way of anyone
suddenly too tuned to everyday events
once hidden in convenient clouds
but now laid bare
as an avocado pit
exposed in half a fruit
staring at the heart of it
and first time seeing it
from head to boot

Still Here

A breeze through the window at my back
now that summer has reached its august stage
is cool, the apple tree outside another window sways
near the purple plum and I, as usual, bring you coffee

and you're still here as the cat leaps from floor to sill
still here as crow caws on her breakfast hunt
still here as the conversation of birds begins again
still here as the scent of cut grass seeps through the screen
and I think of all the reasons you might not be:
ones loaded with fear

Your twin, wan and tiny in her big bed,
slim moon waning, a spent crescent
but you, her spitting image, remains
still here, still here against odds,
waking, dear as the sun, which is here again
rising, still warming, still here because
what seems temporal is everlasting
as the space between now and then

Old Lovers

Two old lovers—
ships beached in the sea of love
in a cove off a bay no storm can reach
lean into each other longing not for past passion
not listening for a poet's speech
just listing, leaning each into each

5

That's It

That's It

I'd mowed. I'd cut and weeded
Tips of fingers earth-inked, I'd seeded

I'd heard our cardinal calling
I'd heard our engines down the valley groaning
coming up, distant, moaning

Hands among dry stems of garlic moving,
like my mother kneeling, devout
but not in church

I'd yanked contentious weeds, insisting,
pulling —this was how I worked:
so much sweat I wore a perspiration shirt

I'd quit and picked my tools up:
shovel rake— and shut the hose off
at the door I took my boots off
smacked them sole to sole to knock the mud off
and turned to see your garden blazing
with inner light in daylight failing
I cracked a beer and sat— amazing!

I watched your garden's still fires burning
it's orange lilies burning
its incandescent red & purple gladiolas burning
its spiky flush of bee balm burning
rose campion bursting in the burning
sparking coral bell and yellow lupine burning
moonbeam coreopsis burning
all in   all on   all still   all lit
until the mountain's shadow eased the fire's edge off
and petal embers in its dying spit
as if some hand had turned a dimmer of the sun
to gently cauterize the done
to douse the blaze
to ease the day off
to say, *that's it*

Hawks

east or west down the trail in fog
the bark of a distant dog

a meadow rolls off in that cloak
in its breast the cleft of a brook

deciduous trees to the north
a hawk in the fifth or the fourth

scans for the twitch of a meal
not a stitch of remorse will it feel

as it falls on its prey like a bomb
with cold indifferent aplomb

there are such people who prey
on an earth created this way

ODDER STILL

A Vase of Queen Anne's Lace

white dust from a vase
of Queen Ann's Lace
settles on a table
upon the golden oak
(in spots as dark as sable)
in sunlight

    soaked
    in moonlight's
    graces

drenched in secondhand love
in platinum, and in shadows
where everything begins

    from where it's spun
    to where it goes
    and spins

Gaia

three sparrows in an arbor vitae
whose mouths—want, need and live
gape as soon as mother comes with grub

a trio of capacious hollows
swallow everything she gives

we watch from near the purple yarrow
in the shade of a magnolia tree

we see the way she waits on guard
outside the shrub

for her the way is canny, straight and narrow,
her love is unencumbered by the verb to be

The Hunter

I hike up a hill at a clip
to keep this heart alive

Orion's over my left shoulder
with arms raised always
in his almost-never-ending black
place in the sky immersed in
blazing stars in utter space

Skirting single Cheryl's
I wonder again, what is it she does
In summer her shingled ranch
is ablaze with lilies
She works them with a goofy hat
stopping now and then to swab sweat

I watch while beyond the blue
the Hunter stands with his legs apart
"I'll live near forever," he mocks,
and his belt-stars testify

I pick the pace up now and feel
the suck of cool air into my lungs
At the top of the hill the road's crown
is the pate of a disturbed
menace standing; straining
beneath asphalt; bending it up

A cleat-pocked phone pole's
draped lifeline-wires
disappear into the dark

An old sugar maple's there too,
its cleft bark bathed in amber sodium vapor,
bare limbs a wild, strobed lattice
moving at my pace as I pass

While the Hunter in the background,
knees ever sprung for action
perseverates for years and years,
I whistle past the graveyard popping Lipitor

Aftermath

Two weeks back the river came through
on a tear to the sea. Tree trunks
slid beneath the arched bridge on brown swells

A small shop pirouetted off piers,
floated downstream and lodged against
the gates of the dam

Cellars crammed with silt and whatever the river'd
sucked from cesspools, gardens of summer moons,
from landfills and barns— earth and offal
came down through here and left its haul
along its banks, in basements, on streets

Field corn, high enough the day before
when its cobbed yield might have grinned yellow
from white plates until the hurricane laid it low—
its ranks of stalks pulled flat by the river's winnowing rake
lays supine as a man after a sweet or savage life
lies still before the sweep of the sea

Bark

---

three deer at my tomatoes
glance up the hill to the house
two adolescents and a doe

they'll scour the woods this winter
        foraging until,
when all else is gone,
bark will do

        but under a sun's blaze
on a globe situated so,
perfectly placed to draw springs of blood
from dirt

        with fountains rich
and provident enough to vitalize its dark soil
we wander now in fresh skin coats to browse

to nose for stuff
that makes us spark

now among red tomatoes all's well
as we're oblivious to an age of bark

Band of Saints

walking in his garden
he apologized to his sunflowers,
promising things would change

by all that's right he swore
he'd end his war with the earth
that brings them forth
on stalks thick as trunks
of pine or spruce
upon which heads bright and big
turn from north, leaves spread
like psalms of singing hands
in close rows of six foot stems
 —a wall solid as the barn-side east
its shadow-fall upon baptisia—
soil, space, each umber face and gold corolla
together a mute *coro de oro* true
as a band of saints to which he
genuflects and greets

Dead Zone

You are sequestered in water
I am confined by the air

You are scaly and finny
I am soft-skinned and fair

I am a reader of volumes
You are a swimmer in time

You read the text of the ocean
I tread the sea of my mind

You draw your breath from a liquid
I take mine from a gas

I am as slow as a dimwit
You are exceedingly fast

I know little of coral
You know nothing of trees

You know the feel of a current
I know the touch of a breeze

You seem content to be fishy
I'm seldom content to be man

You take pleasure in isness
I take it however I can

Your limit seems bounded and narrow
I think my limit is none

I die by the bounty I squander
You die by the damage I've done

Geese

the sky's red skin drawn across a beginning
the grass taut with frost, the clarity of the edge of things
as if rendered by an engraver's point—

an irregular V of geese passes
like beads of an animated rosary,
each a honking Hail Mary
a striving prayer
an individual articulating dot

an I-am of
we-are:

we are moving south
we are honking like hell
we are drifting up and down
in a wandering V together
to reach some destination
by a means coded in our cells
by a wisdom unknown
by an accident or lovely intention
on a whim or a want
on an updraft or drawn down
by a turn in the weather

we have been drawn and
are moving on implacably
as life moves

Dignity

in the garden
falling among Pat's lilies
falling too

hummingbird
tiny as a big bee

its red-head harvests,
hovers, not falling, but
falling too, around a starbud
also falling on the fringe
of a galaxy freefalling
amongst what?

hummingbird slingshots to hydrangea
impossible wings against falling
invisibly against falling
determined as one oppressed
not to fall, or fall
of her own choosing
by her own hand, losing
at her own calling

Hazy Moon

Last night I almost hugged the hazy moon,
that crazy bubble in the sky
who is ever entering new phases.

She rose red, round, and huge
as a melon of imagination

She loomed listening to the pine pitch
and birch bark, an ear for the night choir
She tugged
I leaned as she rolled higher

Two hands from the horizon
she pulled in humble as a quarter
levitated and kissed the high limb tips
of a twisted locust tree

For a moment free
in the circle of her gravity
I understood what that chalkball moon
held over me

She hovered like a lover on a balcony
waiting for a star to shoot
She disappeared once each month
leaving the shadow undilute
but she was never faithless

Always she returned
sweet as an arc of cantaloupe
billowing like a parachute,
calling to the oceans in their cells

reaching down to the tips
of the deepest roots
coaxing up through the tender stems
of slender shoots
dragging even through the leather hearts
of old galoots
the purest waters of the poorest wells

Light

constant friend
who sets the pace of the day
depending upon content

the day is short or long,
but light's oblivious to duration
and so is most content

from every place she leaves
to every place she goes
light comes (it might be said)
religiously and faithfully
tells us what she knows

mornings came and went
in galaxies we will never see
(distances that supersede
even her swift speed
keep them the dark)
yet, constantly, she made way in time
—a spark arcing through dust and nebulae

as supernova atoms shattered
she set off from star clusters
maintaining, like a metronome,
the pulse of mind-with-matter
illuminating every wall upon which
her photons splattered
perturbing all with all the force
her waves could muster,
serving me, at last
the brilliance of the earth
upon a solar platter

Seeding

seeding in a cloud of black flies
kneeling and swatting

lettuce seeds drop
small and humble as asterisks
noting other thoughts of legends
of a universe ripe with protein
and photosynthesis

of leaves enfolded on dinner plates
being lifted by forks slicked with oil and vinegar,
garnished with mystery

crisp sweet and fresh as the day of
Let there be light

Weekend in the Garden of My Sixties

Two days behind a roto-tiller panting like a spent mutt
you get to meditating on poor Yorick's skull

Barely holding back the stallions of a Briggs and Stratton
you smell the nearness of becoming void and null

You wonder how's my ticker doing
and will I soon be caving in a final bow?

You consider, I could suddenly be toodle-looing
I could be tumbling headlong into dirt right now

You wonder then-if the world will matter
You wonder, how deep's this mine?

You wonder how far your dust might scatter
You wonder how much longer the juice will crackle
down and up your spine

Odder Still

Hummingbird Acetylene

the turquoise flame of a hummingbird's head
is a blazing torch of acetylene

burning, as when my father put a welding tip to steel
joining parts of his world with the bluegreen flame
he held between

this hummingbird burns in afternoon light
at the mouth of a flower in god's machine

jabbing her tip at a perfect hour
joining her flame to mine
in a darting iridescent sheen

Who'd Ruin That?

In November 2012, **Nature** *published a commentary by
financier and environmental philanthropist Jeremy
Grantham urging scientists to join (in protest) . . . and
'be arrested if necessary', because climate change 'is not
only the crisis of your lives – it is also the crisis of our
species' existence' ".*

don't say we can't keep doing this
because we can   —until we can't
or won't

nature slams a door
some things cannot supplant the essence
of that which we adore
or don't

just tonight,
walking on a vast tar floor—
the inverse moat
around a big box store,
there not to keep the other out,
but to ease the other into spending more

—oddly there, and just tonight
a once-in-a-lifetime brilliant sky
had stopped me cold
—clouds relaxed. They sprawled, rear-lit,
edged in gold leaf born of an almost by-gone sun
now below the mountain west
but still shattering the grown-old day
in a blazing blue-green mirror of
spacious light

who'd ruin that?
we might

Song Behind a Rear-Tined Tiller

<hr>

They believed consciousness resided in the heart

Aristotle believed this, and the Egyptians
who scooped out dead Pharaoh's brain
through his nose with a spoon
and stuffed his skull with rags assuring
he would not be thinking in the other world
to which he'd travel by long boat
being wrapped in cloth, speechless, in gold supine,
embarked with a breathless retinue of slaves
through the hole at the end of the earth
to a place far in imagination

Here and now sunlight climbs a trellis of trees
along a rail line on which, at irregular intervals,
a freight comes dragging coal behind three engines
or hauls boxcars labeled *J.B. Hunt,*
or pulls chains of steel cubes and chemical tanks
heavy with the inventions of consciousness,
some inscribed with graffiti sprayed by
a deft hand in bold letters, in colors
set with a master's touch

tuned to the tones of heart and brain
while the smell of blue-grey diesel
sparks a synapse between beats
and one step follows another
behind a rear-tined tiller
as I urge a throttle

Who knows who sings
through what instrument
–did Aristotle?

Strawberry Moon

The Algonquin tribes knew this moon as the
time to gather ripening strawberries
*   –Old Farmer's Almanac*

I read you, Strawberry Moon
you pull the sea in the summer
More than two hundred thousand miles
I see your reach is so long

Your arm of gravity, your face of sunlight at midnight
they hold me too

But in the moon when the deer shed their horns
and the top of the world has leaned a little away from the sun
the colder night who has an edge on his voice
who cares so little for growing things
will make it seem like you'll break
unless you remember the heat
of the Strawberry Moon

I'm with you, Strawberry Moon
I'm dark here down in your shadows
which move their edges like steel
when you're full and spilling silver on me

Your arm of gravity, your face of sunlight at midnight
they hold me too

Blink

In a blink the sun comes up
over mountains sublime
and the sea laps it's brim like a pup

regal elms come and go
splayed trunks broken by blight
limbs corrupt

future and past collide
winds whistle side by side
bodies touch and often burn up

wars rage
scriptures are taught
good and bad divide
killers are caught
doors open doors shut

in a blink they say
never the twain shall meet
but twains meet
even poor men acquire like Tut
and beast and beauty wed,
though news of a split soon spreads:
Truth Divorced By Such-and-Such
the tabloids eat it up

notions of right and wrong are cinched
in tiny minds that grasp and clinch
and root and rut

love is made
bodies entwine
hate's kicked on its ass so hard
it can't get up

mountains move
the earth erupts
promises are kept
and given up
and odes and fugues
make offers
we shouldn't refuse,
they demand
we not interrupt

in a blink
all of us know
but no one agrees
if mountains are mountains
and trees are trees
if sky is sky
if mud is mud
if wine's just wine
if blood's just blood
either way
in a blink

in a blink
we drink
it up

Tabula Rasas

In my town
new mothers spring up like weeds.
They roll fold-up strollers
along Bridge Street or
tote sleeping babes that loll like
tot marsupials in sacks
strapped across breasts:
gene parachutes
trussed over shoulders
and buckled in back.
A moment ago
these moms were tot
marsupials too.
Now, out of nowhere–
ignorant as saints or
immune to despair, or both–
they come toting or pushing
mute futures as if headlines
had no place in their dreams;
as if their children
were joyful counterweights
to the evening news,
brimming with hope as tabula rasas,
promising as a new day.

Cat Dance Music

Dance!

Delphiniums winddance
with phlox in Pat's garden
they sway in quiet concord
rooted in motion

dancing's a vital sign of endless youth
even my grandmothers danced
one danced to accordianed polkas
corseted cantilevered bosom bouncing
the other jigged across her chicken yard
with handfuls of eggs having just left her hens
without yield, acting goofy for a camera

I once danced with abandon
to big-holed 45s
spun by a DJ, Jocko
who sent four-part doowop through my radio:
the Prisonaires the Cadillacs the Moonglows

When was the last time I danced with abandon?
How did I do that beautiful thing?

It's best to dance with others, real gurus say
It's lonely dancing with a mirror

leading and following in one motion,
thinking breaking it would be bad luck

our cats dance to deep cat vibrations always
alert as —*cats*
to music far beyond our ears:
cat dance music

Zorba knew. Have you seen
Quinn, the Greek, dance?
Felt life spring in rhythms?
Watched it prance on toes to a bouzouki
even in the clutch of despair?

Never forget how to dance
All innocents dance
Only the troubled are still

Past Prime

Knowing I once could whip
two 2 by 12 by 12s
to shoulder height
from a ground-level stack
without ripping a ligament;
or haul two sheets of drywall
at a time across a room alone
without reaching for the liniment,
I'm pissed at being humbled
by a mere rock-salt sack
I strain to lift and lug
and spread so as not to slip
and be laid up with a broken hip

Making a Home

what I think over and over
eventually I do

I've been teaching body all along
to dance the cantos of my thoughts
how can it not do what it learns?

innocence seeps away
through the interstices of neglect

if I have not built a room
to house a pure idea
it will move on to a better man
and leave my vacant skull to host
what loathes a vacuum

First Zucchini

Today I spied our first zucchini
which has followed its saffron flower
like a compliant stud swelling in shade
within a forest of coarse stubbled stems
under a tent of broad leaves
green as the second color of Christmas
a nativity here of the first order
all six inches of it looking to a future of sacrifice
in a sauté mingled with garlic and onions
growing now in nature's nest
at the whim of god,
for want of a satisfying
rational explanation

Last Zucchini

But for two still-green plants
the zucchini have been ripped up

a heap of hollow stalks and yellow leaves
lies at the end of their once-lush row

the reaper's been through
zucchini day is done

The sun-starved weeds that hunkered tenuously
under the zuke's broad fronds sprout now
in the short late sun unaware of their
cramped circumstances: the late hour,
the short days, the persistence of cosmic
revolutions, the meaning of the cant of axes:
the pinch of relativity—

Just 10 weeks ago I wrote of the first zucchini
a compliant stud swelling in shade I said,
bound for succulent sacrifice in a sauté
and I spoke true—we did savor sun

but now, from one of two remnant plants,
I pluck Mr. Last without remorse hoping

that in this or some other inevitable revolution
in one certain approaching autumn or another

I'll be attuned enough to know
what it means to be myself
matter-of-factly plucked

6

There For Me

There for Me

When someone we love is feeling other-coast lonely
and troubled by one of the ten-thousand things that occur
she'll sometimes say,

I know. I know you're both there for me,
but it'd be nice if someone were, right now, here for me

And I say, I know, because
    there for me
is not as everyday wonderful as
    here for me

    therefore we
are sometimes sad for Me, but

    hear! for Me
is still not in so dark a place

as long as
    they're for me

Into the Wind

—for George D.

You meet a man through a poetry swap
and know by the heft of his words
—how they lift and place the things
that need to be said—
that if you'd known him otherwise
you might have been friends
Then, when you hear he's disappeared
and his book is on the table
still as the moment he left
you make what you can of
what's been missed

—you read
and send his thoughts
loudly into the wind

Knee-deep as Leaves

—on an email from H.

in a wired java shop today
among caffeinators I
received a poem from a friend
who I've know since
before I understood friendship
but now I do
and appreciate his calling me
into the world of this poem
(which is not his, but his
anyway in that he saw the truth in it
and supposed that I might too)

With thanks it joins all the other truths
that have blown against my door
piled now knee deep as leaves
(though less brittle) in fall

Punch Line and Photons

—talking with W. about our elder mothers'
senses of humor

what's the difference between
humor and light?

even in gloomy shuttered rooms
beams successfully invade
through impossible slits
and penetrate wherever
shadows rule

a joke, a laugh,
a silly recollection,
and disease for a instant
disappears

punch lines and photons,
comedians and brilliant suns
bring us as close to god
as anyone need be

Punctuation

Period—

With this almost inconspicuous dot I wrap things up.
Bring all pleasures to an end. Call it off.
There's a tiny tidiness to it, but the muscle of
cessation too —It can stop a truck.

Question Mark—

With this sinuous hook I pop a question
whenever I want to reach outside the box I'm in:
Why God, for instance?
Or how come these crows do not give ground
but stand and glare as if they owned this field
of mine and me?
How deeply down are they aware?
How far under do they stare?
How much more of something do they see?

Comma—

With this tadpoled period I may pause a second,
swimming among multitudes noting and naming.
Mesmerized by its breath-taking tail I rest,
then go on expanding and elucidating,
although in this case of hesitating
I've nothing more to say and no one's waiting anyway
except for future anthropologists
nosing round and carbon dating

But wait, there's more, With comma's versatility
I may string ten thousand things like beads
listing names of every city in the world, every lover,
their triumphs, dreams and classic poses
or as the evening closes, I may breathe mid-sentence
and signify I've thought of something else:
alyssum, phlox, hydrangea, roses
And finally, to show how much you mean to me, my friend,
I'll set your name apart with two of these for rapt attention
until I'm ended with that dot I mentioned.

Rapprochement

Just wondering
if worlds seen from a distance
are really smaller than they are

Could it be that when we sleep
the world we leave goes on without us

Maybe you remember the old days too
when greenhorns multiplied their joys
and were thoughtless as a new moon

Is it possible that, upstairs, everything is seen
through a rose window bright as Venus
or is there nothing to be seen between us

Perhaps you needed to spend some years
on an island being tuned

You thought I might be
shoveling snow this morning
on the cusp of spring

I wanted to ask if maybes still exist
or if tomorrow is so sure a thing

So, are you still counting coup
on the enemies of the morning dew

Haven't heard, so I thought I'd tell a new tale
one of thoughts that may never have been played,
thoughts naked as new babes born today

Have you noticed something odd?
Nothing ever changes but the color
of the feather in the hat band of god

Could I
ask

Would you
answer

What the
fuck

Why the unworn soles of shoes
on the feet of the dancer?

When did you say you last caught
glimpses of the ghosts you fought

You didn't say, but I suspect
you're still stuffed with words,
a cornucopia of clever twists
in our alphabet

Possibly it's a mistake,
but even god is not perfectly awake

For what it's worth breakfast's the best meal of the day—
the sun's a fresh egg, the clouds white albumin
—ahead? a day with lots of space to stew in

Guess I could just jot something
resembling our bridges of contention
with their steel beams and delicate
cables of suspension

If it's not too much to ask
(the paper being so unreliable these days
and television a joke),
how's the weather?

Fine —and yours?
As fine, I hope

The Swing

—to the kids I've swung

Every year from early May to harvest moon
I'm back and forth behind my Deere

I cut the crabgrass yard I call my lawn
It's weekly done if we've had monsoon

If it's dry as a bone I get a week-or-so reprieve, but
every time my mower sings I face the swing

The swing's a wood slab on a nylon rope
hung on a high birch branch over a side yard slope

–the slope is smooth and slight
the rope is blue and white

Underneath, a spot once brown and bare
was scuffed by feet that grazed it there
from year to year to year to year

Small feet swung and scuffed it there
from year to year to year to year

Now the grass beneath the swing's
a pretty, plush but poignant green

Time Enough

A clock and you and me alone in a room with time
to settle accounts, still time enough to bare and binge,
to rewrite ends, swapping tales that make us cringe,
some so fierce and hot they make our memory singe

The clock and I are willing but the flesh is weak,
—I worry what the wound in you might speak

Before the snow of last night's furies melt
love would not be a bad wrap, please
tell me what you felt

I see crystals heaped three inches deep
on a branch of the Magnolia tree
where they thaw and drop for you and me

Typo

---

*—on being corrected by my wife
for a misspelled Wednesday*

ok, ok, in fact Wedneaday is a new day
(don't we need one every once in a while?)

it comes after Toodleday
and is exactly one day before Thurbleday
which itself precedes Fryday
which is closely followed by Shatterday
(but not too intimately lest we have a birthday incident
and wind up with a tiny, odd little day
appropriately called Sonday — or Daughterday
depending upon X or Y)

in any case, after Shatterday comes Shunday
—a day dedicated to dissing anyone
who shattered your dreams on Shatterday
(hopefully not me)

finally we come full circle to the day before Toodleday,
Mindy, who is not really a day at all
but comes between Shunday and Toodleday
(if she has an artful and tender lover
with a day off)

Now I Know What He Meant

—I'll have that done in no time,
my father would say

I'm in the midst of a moon
(as the Lenape called them)
dead center. It's Thursday
dead center, too, of the week

I'm at the pinpoint of noon poised
precisely at the day's fulcrum
just thirty seconds into the minute
at point five Oh! of that second

and a breeze blows

across my cheek

which the sun warms

in no time

Again

My father, at the kitchen table,
in a rare expression of mystery,
said, *I think life is a cycle*
But he was not a mystical man to me,
nose to the grindstone he ground
day after day, pressed
by incessant work, bound
to contingencies
like Sisyphus to his stone
linearly, but uphill
in his black boots and socks
his blue shirt and pants
cinched with a black belt,
sometimes a fedora,
often a smile through
cigarette-clinched lips,
he trucked on (unbeknownst to me,
and despite his flat trajectory)
mulling over vicissitudes,
contemplating repetitions,
weighing the properties of circles,
as does any common philosopher
hoping to unravel the hiddeness
under blood and bone,
coming to the conclusion
that to begin again
was the only thing that made sense
to him

Small Stones

Take small stones
and imagining their history
hold them

Let the sediment fall
and waiting until there is
no more mud
take what you see

You'll remember how they split
in violent earthly fits
in tempers of steam
before the coming of ears

You'll see them fall
as you fell from your father
like chips
into the soft cup of your mother's hand
and from there into your own

Hold to their shapes
and you'll feel the suck of your lungs
filling their caves
with northern January breath

Building a Stupa

Assemble a tower for Buddha and watch it fall —Anon

I stack stones carefully
finding their centers of gravity
the lump of one fitting the nook of another
building a precarious tower in the grass
near the flowering purple plum
under a clear sky with a breeze
catching the nape of my neck
mussing my gray crown of hair
as dad once did with his hand
reaching across the seat
as we drove somewhere

7

Victor Borge
and the Player Piano

Victor Borge and the Player Piano

One day when we lived on Oak
my father came home with a white piano
big and heavy as a horse that had
two large pedals under its keys which
if you placed a paper roll called Lady of Spain
between two spindles behind a sliding door
above the keys like a wood block in a lathe
and pumped with both feet the avatar
of Victor Borge would come and sit and play
blacks and ivories (some like bad teeth)
succumbing to the ghosts of his hands
as you watched ascending and descending
perforations in the roll's paper
pass over the horizontal row of holes
in the smooth brass bar at eye level
like flocks of geese coming and going
the pattern of perforations sliding from
top roll to bottom orchestrating the piano's
robot rendition of Lady of Spain
while Borge slap-sticked and cracked-wise
seated right where you sat
your fingers floating over the keys
performing furious air arpeggios until you
dropped off the end of your seat to the floor
pretending to be that slapstick funny man
with fingers as facile
in the adult manner of a brilliant
Danish clown

Blue Wheel Barrow

— a nod to poet, Dr. W.C. Williams

so much depends
upon

a blue wheel
barrow

if it were
red

I might have been a
doctor-poet

and still live in
Paterson

only this time with white
chickens

in the
rain

Girl on Trapeze

—vignette in a windshield

young girl on a curb
waiting for a green
it comes, she goes, head down
checking out the cut of her jeans:
how they lay across her shoes;
the way the inseams hug her firm thighs;
the fine, faded blues

sweet on self
she imagines an approaching guy
sees what she eyes
(sees himself as her squeeze)
Him, turned on
Her, self pleased

she smiles raises head reins eyes
veers right wields keys
and swings into her car
with beautiful and satisfied
greatest of ease

Halberg's Rooster

Up the road
Halberg's rooster,
descendent of dinosuars,
croaks his 4 syllable hello to the sun
as mighty We,
dumb as rooster ancestry,
imagine we shall always be

Icon

I received a snap of Duke the Dog
in which Duke, in radiant atmosphere, stands
quintessentially dog-like:
     open-mouthed lolling tongue,
four-square
paws planted in green earth
     expectant
poised to please   Christ-like
in halo mist   silent   light   still
     aware

I'm yours, he barks, standing by.
Throw that last stick now
before I mount this brilliant torch
and rise to sit at dad's right paw:
my father King who (tooth and claw)
salutes every risen pooch from
dog-heaven's porch

for though it's mysteriously odd
dog spelled backward is always god

Ignorant Explorers

in what seems void are corridors:
invisible filaments in gravity's net
between planets, suns, moons,
meteors, dust—

channels
in networks of love among us

through them we move
first in flame machines
burning hydrogen, smoldering lust
to come hopefully unspent upon
some new shore anywhere but here

anywhere but in boredom
anywhere but in the best place:
the den the lair the home the nest
the sanctum cloister cave the rest

anywhere but the wholly familiar
being such bold and
ignorant explorers

More Splintered Than Common Sense

*As a layman, I would now say, I think we have it. It's an
historic milestone today. I think we can all be proud and happy.
       —CERN director-general Rolf-Dieter Heuer,
         upon discovery of the long sought-after
         Higgs Boson, 4/7/2012*

Having heard hints
of a never-before-seen particle
my day becomes new
the blue day is further fractured

What were small thoughts become
more pint-sized then the nonsense
of politicians: smaller even
than the bits of stained tile mosaic
under my feet beneath
a urinal

I'm told this is the much-sought-after
Higgs boson I've been chasing
my whole life, looking for it between
the pillows of my couch where I
often find keys and dimes.
Hope surged when I heard the news
my tomatoes perked green
their leaves and tiny blossoms
pulling in new knowledge
and light

Scientists muse: this particle
could be a new force of nature,
beyond sex perhaps;
maybe greater than greed

Who knows what new brick of the cosmos
they've found in their accelerator
in unexpected bumps in jets
of colliding particles noted
while they sipped Starbucks
as the white dust of a sugared torus
settled upon the lapels of their lab coats
and the macro-world fragmented
simultaneously with the micro
into something even more splintered
than common sense

My Religious Life

The Tao that can be thought of is not the real Tao;
therefore the Tao that can be spoken is not real either;
so, the Tao that can be named is likewise no thing too.
—Lao Tzu, sort of

I was Catholic,
but was not universal enough
when I was.

I was Protestant,
but did not protest enough
when I was.

I was a Transcendental Meditationist,
but was not transcendent enough
when I was.

I was a dilettante Buddhist,
but (unlike the lotus) I failed to bud
when I was.

Now as a Taoist
in an inscrutable plan
I'm most content, because
it's nothing I can really talk about
if I am.

Red Cardinal

Today I spied a red cardinal
perched on the branch of a birch
regal as any red Cardinal
perched in a branch of a church.

Hey, I say, lovely red, redbird
where is it you come from?
He sang in his red, red cardinal voice,
I was born where this song is sung.

Where'd that be little bird? Tell me.
I really need to know.
But what good to tell such an obvious thing
to a man who prevaricates so?

And the cardinal dipped
(as Cardinals bow
before a cardinal rule)

and flew off then
to a sky or a church
and ditched this cardinal fool.

The Problem of Time

then was now once
while now is always
the train leaving the station

and Is (itself) is pretty much
a matter of interpretation
as murky as the dilemma:
to be or not to— which was
well explored long before today

(today being exactly when
Hamlet was written anyway)

Tomorrow maybe I'll figure it all out,
though by then it'll be almost yesterday again

which before tick has tocked will
seem like a month or two ago
or year or even an eon or so,
which it probably is
for all I know

To Roof

Ah, to put a roofing spade
to desiccated shingles

To lean upon the spade-handle's end
leveraging stubborn nails
from their impacted seats

To wrench my back

To abrade my bleeding hands again
stroking the asphalt's pebbled face

To fight a wind while laying felt
which, like Ahab's sails, would whisk me
to a mad roofer's end

To slam my thumb once more

To slash my hands with flashing
imagining the course of rainwater
flowing down a 4 square deck—
placing aluminum just so
as if I could plumb
a droplet's depth

To race the advance of a front

To look skyward anxious
under gathering clouds

To become so unfocused in haste
my courses, like the venal
schemes of politicians, veer off
disordered and untrue
leaving poor substrate constituents
vulnerable to a deluge

Ah, but then, at last,
to button it up

To take the staging down
and store the ladder

To pack the tools and,
eye-balling the shingled slope,
wax smug

To hope again I'd out-danced
natural law
To think I'd punked Poseidon
(who pelts my roof with rain and hail)

To stride off then, self-satisfied
and jam my foot into a roofing nail

Möbius Trick

Know what history is?

God's Möbius trick
in which s/he flips the strip of time
and joins its ends upside down
which does much to explain
the recurrence of the dumb shit
of man's delights in sight and sound
which every century and day
comes round comes round
comes round comes round

Hormones in Love

Only one can have this thought
Did you think your thoughts were mine?

We lie apart as close as this:
thinking   still   alone   combined

Two skulls each with a budding brain
Two "I"s distant as two moons
catching light from somewhere else
too bright to be too far, and soon

we come together touch and kiss
we think there is no more than this
we think we think the self-same thoughts
—but pleasure's not the same as bliss

We come together, kiss and touch
We think, this close is not too much
And though we dream that we are one
—embrace is not the same as *clutch*

8

Tiny Megalomaniacs

Tiny Megalomaniacs

being good
you must take responsibility for everything
and credit for nothing
otherwise you slide down
a slippery slope at an accelerating clip
until you're taking credit for everything
and responsibility for zip

just a short slip down that slope
you've already sloughed goodness
many times like snake skin
for the sake of some small gain
some little leverage, some edge, some in
elbowing out some less able
contestant in Darwin's world
to gain what turns out to be
a plot of worthless sand
by means of tiny sins

it's tough, discernment's not easy
in the muddle of desire
everything you think you require is righteous
so you turn to gods that fan that fire
you whisper prayers into corners first
then, picking up a head of steam,
you're bellowing your righteousness from peaks
as your minions mutter lies up and down mean streets
and many bubbles burst

but more often than not you don't get that far
you settle for a provincial fiefdom
running a big firm or corner bar,
equally worthy jobs
if your heart's in the right place
and you understand the limits of all
and know you're in this universe
under an umbrella of chance,
lucky to be small
and know you have just a tiny part
in the making of this
curious dance

Problematica

*"Many life forms are so hard to categorize that (scientists)
call these organisms the 'Problematica.'"*
> —*from:* Scatter, Adapt and Remember:
> How Humans Will Survive a Mass Extinction,
> *by Annalee Newitz*

Here we are, never still, casting lines
upstream like fly fishers toward sources
teeming with what came first
hooking what we can, reeling it in
holding it before our minds eye smiling,
snapshotting bizarre Cambrian trophies
placing ourselves at the daisy chain's end
hoping not to be rolled over or under
by our own cleverness, extinct as past
Problematica looking odd and grotesque
to future fishers —as uncategorizable
as the dead husks of Amebelodon
whose strange tusks are the only ruts
they've left in rutted time

Safe

Before I built a wall I'd ask to know
What I was walling in or walling out
          —Robert Frost, Mending Wall

I'm safe
I've locked myself in
You're here and safe too
Through the barred window of this box
the world has changed, grown more lovely

I savor its barred beauty more
as I recall it close at hand

Now unattainable it seems exquisite
or, I see now how exquisite it has always been

But we're safe now from its predations
bounded and safe

look, out there, the honeysuckle,
remember its scent?

Down to the Bone

...and then I heard
"ring of bone" where
ring is what a
bell does
　　　　—Lew Welch

If I could un-ring certain bells and un-wind time I
would, but can't, so instead, I'll just ride this bucket
of bones till the wheels fly off; till ball-joints grind
and drop from sockets; till this xylophone of ribs
riffs the music of the spheres; until my funny bone
tells it's last joke; till my shoulder blades cleave the
universe in two and find the nut within; until I'm
hipper than both hips and happier; till I'm savvy at
last, slicker than elbow grease, and mute as a smart
metatarsal; until I'm wiser than a thought-stuffed
skull; until I knee-cap my inner sonofabitch to stop
his useless jawin' so I can hear one clear day
resound off tiny anvils and ride the lyrical looped
song of a backyard bird round Lew Welch's ring of
bone.

Instead...
I'll just splint what needs splinting
right here at home.

The Frequency of Error

---

*... the "Law of Frequency of Error" ... would have been
personified by the Greeks and deified, if they had known
of it. It reigns ... amidst the wildest confusion. The huger
the mob, the greater the anarchy, the more perfect is its
sway. It is the supreme law of Unreason.*
  —Victorian statistician Francis Galton

The frequency of error
is not a count of radio waves
or of an articulation of sound
expanding from me to you
through space with
ample atmosphere
The frequency of error
is the number of times,
in the fog of Me,
I've stumbled into doors
and bashed my head
on low-hanging branches
of the tree-of-knowledge-
of-good-and-evil
yet against all odds
have lived to tell the tale

The frequency of error
is not a dulcet wave,
but a mob of mad particles
which routs the better angels of my nature
hammering them with crude clubs
made by my own hand
in fits of id

Civilization

*"Civilization" is the soothing notion that in it natural
callousness has been successfully quarantined.*
        —Roshi Bob

A cat on the center pillow of a couch
looks out through windows facing south
with the fierce frustration of an indoor cat
who preys through glass

The squalor of first spring just after the snow has passed
fills her gaze, pierces drabness for anything that moves
beyond the breezy animation of pine limbs and spruce—
quick jerk or dart of something sentient on the loose
which, unlike a couch cat, lives with the threat of spacious freedom,
in the wind, on the prowl without the leash of civil cover,
who scuttles among the hungry with a life as long as its cunning
who's liberty is only cramped by the cunning liberty of others

9

What Is Leaving?

What is Leaving?

gust
    air once here goes
    to fill a vacuum there
dusk
    the sun no more,
    is behind mañana's door

I can't recall my last glimpse of you
You went
I'm living your wake

And here comes Go again
blazing her trail of tears
while Gone is close behind
sweeping footprints with a green pine bough
from Going's dust as I pine now

Getting to Know You

I'm getting to know you who came
with the first Archaeon's spark

Everything was new then, even you, you
parenthetical tail of vital events, you
old telegraphic protoplasmic stop, you
callous caboose bringing up the rear of trains
of eloquent clauses, fertile words,
grunts and final remains, you
small but lethal punctuational dot

You came on the scene with the first cell-knots waiting
You stood in the dark as first hearts began beating
In celebrations of birth you grabbed orchestra seating
At wakes you confirmed your ruthless deleting

Never kind to lovers you roamed the earth like a shade
two-stepping with light —its dissembling side:
what it made you unmade

Here it comes! Alarms went out
when your coughing heralds came through
making it clear you'd arrive to nullify anything new

Alone in your shadow lovers wept
embracing only the smoke they'd kept
of the flame you'd snuffed before you left

On the Difficult Terminal Illness
of a Beloved
(art, science, being)

---

*"Despite its mystic chic the square root of pi is
indeterminate and makes no sense, like many other things."*
  –Roshi Bob

Black holes, Big Bang, Bada Bing,
quantum space, worm holes, theory of strings;
space is a smorgasbord of metaphors of things

Inside out, upside down, left and right,
geometry, calculus, depth and height;
Pythagoras' spheres all sing in the dead of night

Who went where? What was what? Which was when?
Fortune and fame, persecution and plot, since time began
history alliterates again and again

Two plus two, me less you, nine times nine,
the square root of pi, theorems and proofs, the curve of a sine;
math is a simile for the shape of time

Bacteria, wisteria, DNA,
diphtheria, alstroemeria, the end of days;
biology's an accident of come-what-mays

Mirror

—on my mother's birthday

Under cover of light the moon disappears
just like that, following my mother
travelling not by casket but
instead by memory and dream
(alike as death and birth), so alike
there's just this mirror between them

Whatcham'callit

She's dead, he said
So's he, said she

Kicked the bucket, he said
Bought the farm, said she

Under the clover, he said
Crossed over, said she

Iced with a heater, he said
Sleeps with the fishes, said she

Taken for a little ride, he said
Gone to the other side, said she

Flat-lined, he said
Out of mind, said she

To a better place, he said
By heaven's grace, said she

Under the sod, he said
To be with God, said she

To Paradise? he said
Would be nice, said she

Could it be? he said
Could it not? said she

A Cornucopia of Elegies

In the beginning was the word —the logos—
the indwelling logic, the rational order of things

clear as time when the air was green
and tenderfeet knew the ballet of beginning

—a tern-like teen on one leg
in the surf by a sea

—a swift on a draft of blinks
in the hour of sometime-but-not-now

time is a cornucopia of elegies,
the master of poets complicit
since the word became flesh

The Tongues of his Black Boots Say

as my father sleeps the world goes on
his work boots are by the door
he left them there unlaced
the right run down at the heel
the left's toe scuffed
his blue shirt hangs on a hook
wrinkled below the belt line
where every morning
its tails were tucked
there's no forgiveness in pasts
just now and here, defeat
is the hardest epiphany
the tongues of his
black boots say

10

—

Making Way

Making Way

—Narragansett Bay —1960, first time to sea

we part from the dock
slow as disengaging lovers
one landlocked, the other a
floater who won't be
kept at bay

the diminishing pier slides back
its bollards and planks deploy
to some other place not here
—to a distancing otherworld

the tether breaks
as stern-first we pass the
channel buoy

> *Quarter back, the OD says.*
> *Quarter back, aye sir,*

and we slip away

> *Steer two one zero, half ahead.*
> *Two one zero, half ahead, aye sir*

and we slow-slide down
the gleaming bay

the sun's so keen it indicates
a tern on the roof of a big estate
a half mile away
atop its long lawn hill
off the starboard bow
which slopes down clear
through the wind-wove air
to a point where jades meet blues
                —which passes now
as we part the sea while
making way

further south the sea's first chops
begin to unsettle our sheltered
adolescent cruise

near the harbor mouth all decks
rise then make their first
supplicating bows to whatever
god it is who intervenes
to call-off wrecks
     —we're juggled gently first in
Neptune's law as
pitches rolls & heaves
meet yaws

gray billows diesel from our raked stacks
Halyards snap against the mast's steel
Gulls abundantly rise & reel
over the white chaos of our wake's track

sunlight splinters
into rippled trillions
upon each breaker's
sequined breast
before it folds
in a white rush falling
to the soul percussion
of a bow-wave's
   shush
       shush

Swimming in Spacetime

A short walk from our house
2 minutes tops
the river came through
in a bend at the end of
a short street where
on a small beach
built of slow sand
the river had sloughed
in the shelter of a prominence
upon which a monarch of a
tree stood its four foot trunk
under a green crown
cumulous as the cloud of
dark hair I'd one day wear
I dove down and came up
swimming in space time
in a vacuum when
a bird turned
above my head
and dove too
intent upon a dragonfly
which buzzed through
like the humming bird
with crimson neck
and impossible wings
(as invisible as she
was divine)
swimming in
space time

First Love

I'm falling
for you
falling   falling

the ground's given way
I'm tumbling sprawling

space   space   my mind
my heart   my heart
is in a parabolic arc
without gravity or time

I float   I float
I'm in a massless boat
sailing   sailing

the truth of weight is failing
the truth of sure conclusions gone
I've come apart, I'm
flailing   flailing

up is all around
it's merged with down
if I weren't so glad
I'd certainly be wailing

Odder Still

Dim Bulb on Watch

—North Atlantic, 1960

At sea in a cork
on the back of a frothing bull
grey to infinite horizon
smack in the middle of it
stupid in adventure
bullspit flying everywhere
lurching twenty, thirty feet per leap
pitching, yawing, rolling, falling
it never occurred to me
that I might drown

And so, the dim bulb
of the boy I was
lit my way. And what
dim bulb still does?

Twenty Thousand Six Hundred Eight

I'm out here stacking days as if it were a sport
I'm up to twenty thousand six hundred eight
I sweat memory. I've taken off my shirt,
I'm feeling great. But as I stack
the stack is growing short

I tally what till now I've done

Not far from a stupa
I eye the spot where I'd begun
near an arbor vitae hedge
in a shade of catalpa

I'm looking for bona fide antiques
scented and yellow as old books

On spines of days my curate hands
feel to find the ones with bliss-laced hours
stitched with epiphanic seams
I come upon a few. They're few
and far between

The sun's past high. The pallid moon's
a perfect ghost of round sentinel-still
upon a bald mountain ridge. I think
it might roll down

I breathe honeysuckle and see wisteria
clutch its pole twist up and round

I'd placed the pile with care
so as never to occlude the sun
yet carelessly have thrown
some days upon a previous one
then, too late, gone back to
square them up trying
to undo the done

Lucky Again

---

yesterday today
might never come but
I'm lucky again

it did and here you are
my bulwark against
a stark sea

in the garden you began
years ago in our plot of sand
where little grew but

wild strawberries
close to the ground their
tendrils groping dry earth

we now have hibiscus
with blossoms the size of
dinner plates

and day lilies in colors
of all things that make
death an illusion

for years under your baton
we've sown our sand with
death's stuff

mown grass, dry leaves,
the remnants of meals,
manure of nearby farms

until what was dry is lush
was empty is full
was barren is flush

today tomorrow
may never come but here
you are and I am

lucky again

Acknowledgements

I am grateful to the following people for their encouragement and assistance during the preparation of this book: first, my editor, Mary Lou Dee, who, when I asked if she'd edit this work, enthusiastically and graciously agreed. I so appreciate her time, effort and insights throughout the process. I also want to thank Woody Rudin, Elise Winters, Bill and Nancy Schneberger, Ray Dee, George Cronk and all of *Lena's Basement Press* for their advice and support in making this book possible. Their help and encouragement has been invaluable to me. Further, the advice and guidance of book designer, Andrea Schettino, whose knowledge and skill in the organization and presentation of this book have been exceptional, is much appreciated. I'd also like to thank my long-time friend Harry Walsh who has provided his sensibility and honest appraisal over the years, by letting me know if and when a poem rang true or not. And I'd like to thank Harry for sending the poem that introduced me to Abbas Raza, my editor at *3 Quarks Daily*. Abbas, who gave me an opportunity to share this poetry with a wider readership has also been an important influence in my decision to create this book. In addition, my editors at *The Greenfield Recorder*, Tim Blagg and Justin Abelson, as well as Virginia Ray of the *West County Independent*, who've published my work in various forms, have my gratitude. And finally, I'm grateful to my wife and closest friend Pat, who knows how to call a spade a spade and who has inspired and grounded these poems with her love and honesty.

Acknowledgement is made to the following journals and anthologies in which some of these poems first appeared:

The Christian Science Monitor: "Small Stones"
The Buddhist Poetry Review: "Building a Stupa"
Anon Seven: "Whatcham'callit"
3 Quarks Daily: "A Hole in Vincent's Head", "Dead Zone", "Problematica", and others

Other journals and media sources of written work by Jim Culleny:

Astropoetica, Concise Delights, Muscle and Blood, Five Minute Pieces (chapbook), The Greenfield Recorder, The West County Independent

Broadcast audio essays:

Morning Edition, WFCR, Amherst, MA
NPR, *All Things Considered*

Jim Culleny is also a carpenter, singer, musician and song writer. He resides in Shelburne Falls Massachusetts on a small farm which he and his wife Patricia lovingly tend. He is a father of four daughters and several grandchildren, and it is his family, his parents and siblings, and his daily farm work that inspire some of his most insightful pieces.

Readers who wish to access vocal performances of his poems and songs can link into them at this site:
https://soundcloud.com/jim-culleny

Find Jim's poetry online at *Blink*:
http://jimculleny.wordpress.com

Many thanks for permissions for the images by artists noted below:

The Worker Sisyphus, Sisyphus sculpture and photo
  by Robert Markey
Icon, photo by Kevin Haley & Jeff Grader
Old Lovers, photo by Damian Kane

The Tongues of His Black Boots, drawing by Jim Culleny
Cover image, drawing by Jim Culleny